Start Reading
TOGETHER

Animals in Danger

Anne Faundez

QED Publishing

First published in the UK in 2004 by
QED Publishing
A Quarto Group Company
226 City Road
London, EC1V 2TT

www.qed-publishing.co.uk

A Catalogue record for this book is available from the British Library.

ISBN 1 84538 311 7

Written by Anne Faundez
Designed by Zeta Jones
Editor Hannah Ray
Picture Researcher Joanne Beardwell

Series Consultant Anne Faundez
Creative Director Louise Morley
Editorial Manager Jean Coppendale

Printed and bound in China

Picture credits
Key: t = top, b = bottom, m = middle, c = centre, l = left, r = right

Corbis/Theo Allofs 18–19, 22cl, /Tom Bean 10, /Tom Brakefield 6, /Clem Haagner
17, /Martin Harvey 20–21, /Langevin Jacques 5, /Karen Su 4; **Ecoscene**/Phillip Colla
14–15; **Getty Images** 7; **Still Pictures**/M&C Denis Huot 12–13, /B Lundberg 8, /C
Allan Morgan 16, /H Willcox 9, 22b.

Contents

Under threat

Many types of animal are dying out. These animals are **endangered**.

The animals' homes and food supplies are being destroyed by humans. Humans are also killing large numbers of the animals. This is why the animals become endangered.

In many countries, there are special parks where endangered animals are cared for.

Cheetahs

Cheetahs are the fastest land animals. They live in grassy areas of Africa.

Cheetahs are meat-eaters and eat animals such as hares and antelope.

A baby cheetah is called a cub.

Cubs are grey with long woolly hair along their backs.

Cheetah cubs stay with their mother for about a year.

Cheetahs live for about 10 to 12 years in the wild.

Hazel dormice

Hazel dormice live in Britain. They are a type of mouse.

They have big, sharp front teeth and long furry tails.

8

Hazel dormice sleep, or **hibernate**, in winter. They are also **nocturnal**. This means that they are awake at night and sleep during the day.

Whooping cranes

Whooping cranes have long beaks and long legs. The adult bird is snowy white with a black tip on each wing.

Whooping cranes are the tallest birds in North America. They travel in groups, or **flocks**.

They make a 'whoop' sound when in danger. That is why they are called whooping cranes.

African elephants

12

The African elephant is the world's largest land **mammal**.

Elephants live in a family group, led by an older female.

Elephants eat grass, leaves and bark. They use their tusks for peeling bark off trees, digging and looking for roots.

They live for up to 70 years.

Blue whales

Blue whales are mammals that live in the sea.

The blue whale is the biggest animal in the world. It measures about 30m long.

Blue whales eat large amounts of small, shrimp-like animals called krill.

14

Blue whales have baleen plates instead of teeth. These plates trap the krill but let the water out again.

Blue whales live for about 80 years.

Leatherback turtles

Leatherback turtles are the largest living **reptiles**. They can grow up to 2.5m long. They have a leathery shell and flippers that do not have claws.

Leatherbacks always return to the same beach to lay their eggs. When they have hatched from their eggs, the babies find their own way to the sea.

Yellow-footed rock wallabies

Yellow-footed rock wallabies belong to the kangaroo family.

Wallabies and kangaroos have very strong back legs and hop along the ground, using their tails to balance.

Yellow-footed rock wallabies live in steep and rocky areas of Australia. Their fur matches the colour of the rocks. This is called **camouflage** and makes it very difficult for **predators** to see the wallabies.

Mountain gorillas

Mountain gorillas are the largest type of gorilla. They live in the forests of some African countries.

Mountain gorillas live in groups. The adult male is called a silverback.

The silverback beats his chest to warn the others of danger.

Mountain gorillas' favourite food is bamboo shoots.

Mountain gorillas can live for up to 50 years.

Glossary

camouflage – something that makes an animal look part of its surroundings.

endangered – an animal that is in danger of dying out.

flock – a group of birds.

hibernate – to sleep through the winter until the weather warms up.

mammal – an animal that feeds on its mother's milk.

22

nocturnal – an animal that is active at night, rather than during the day.

predator – an animal that hunts, kills and eats other animals for food.

reptile – a cold-blooded animal such as a snake or a lizard. Often covered in scales.

Index

Carers' and teachers' notes

- Ask your child questions about the picture on the front cover of the book. What does he/she think the book might be about? Read the title to your child. Does he/she still think his/her original guess about the subject of the book is correct?
- Look through the book. Ask your child to choose his/her favourite picture and read that page first. Explain that the pages do not have to be read in order, as they would in a storybook.
- Look at the contents page, the glossary and the index. Explain that these are often found in books which give information (i.e. non-fiction).
- Tell your child that an index helps us to find out where to locate certain information in a book. Look at the order of the words in the index (alphabetical). Sing an alphabet song to remind your child of alphabetical order.
- Point out the words that are in **bold** type. Explain that they are unusual or difficult words and that the glossary helps us to understand what they mean.
- Together, read about the leatherback turtle. Draw around a dinner plate and ask your child to add a head, tail and flippers to the 'shell' and to colour it in. Label your child's picture, asking him/her to help you by suggesting what needs to be labelled.
- Read about the cheetah. Where does it live?
- Use a globe or an atlas to find a map of Africa.
- Which other animals in the book live in Africa?
- Can your child remember how the whooping crane got its name? Can he/she make a 'whooping' noise?
- Can your child jump like a yellow-footed rock wallaby? Can he/she beat his/her chest, just like the silverback gorilla?
- Make a collage of your child's favourite endangered animal using photographs from old magazines, paint, crayons, scraps of fabric and other bits and pieces.